REIMAGINING GROUP WORK

A GUIDE TO CREATIVE FACILITATION

By Bill Crooks and Jackie Mouradian

Written and illustrated by Bill Crooks and Jackie Mouradian
Graphic design: Lindsay Noble

Mosaic Creative
www.mosaiccreative.co.uk
info@mosaiccreative.co.uk
+44 (0) 118 9611359

First edition 2012

ISBN #: 978-1-4716-3351-5

Mosaic Creative are committed to using the visual and performing arts in providing fun and accessible training and resources for the voluntary sector in the UK and overseas.

Contents

Welcome to this Guide

This guide is designed to equip new and experienced facilitators with a range of tools and ideas for making facilitation effective and fun. It draws from our experience of working with groups both in the UK and overseas. Some of the activities in this guide are suitable for workshop situations, while other activities can be used facilitating groups working on a project or an initiative.

Creativity in facilitation requires experimentation with new techniques and approaches. This will inevitably mean taking some risks and learning from mistakes. This guide will give you some resources to help you on your way.

All the best
Bill Crooks and Jackie Mouradian

SECTION ONE

WHAT IS FACILITATION?

What is Facilitation?

Facilitation is the process of taking a group through learning or change in a way that encourages all members of the group to participate.

Facilitation is essential for any community development work, as it is an empowering process and enables groups that are vulnerable or marginalised in any way to gain confidence and realise their potential.

This approach assumes:

- Without each person's knowledge and contribution, the group's ability to understand or respond to a situation may be reduced
- Each person has something unique and valuable to share

Some More Definitions of Facilitation

- Coordinating rather than leading an exercise so that all group members are encouraged to participate in the discussion or activity
- A process of decision making guided by a facilitator who ensures that all affected individuals and groups are involved in a meaningful way and that the decisions are based on their input and made to achieve their mutual interest
- Helping others think through what they want and organise themselves to achieve it
- A collaborative process in which a neutral seeks to assist a group of individuals or other parties to discuss constructively a number of complex, potentially controversial issues
- The art of leading people through processes towards agreed-upon objectives in a manner that encourages participation, ownership and creativity by all those involved
- The process of enabling groups to work cooperatively and effectively
- Engendering an open discussion on a specific set of criteria, where the participants undertake a series of discussions and activities, to ultimately establish a direction
- Enabling a group to focus its energies on its task so that the group can make decisions and promote cooperation among its members. Ensuring that everyone participates, group members are protected and trust is built.

The Role of the Facilitator

- Recognises the strengths and abilities of individual group members and helps them to feel comfortable about sharing their hopes, concerns and ideas
- Supports the group, giving participants confidence in sharing and trying out new ideas
- Values diversity and is sensitive to the different needs and interests of group members. These differences might be due to gender, age, sexuality, disability, race, culture, profession, education, economic or social status
- Leads by example through attitudes, approach and actions

"Facilitation is the art, not of putting ideas into people's heads, but of drawing them out"
Anon

The difference between traditional teaching and facilitation

Teaching

- Sharing of information in one direction
- Presents ideas from the front
- Formal relationship with students

Facilitation

- Sharing of information in several directions
- Facilitator sits with group and encourages discussion
- Facilitator is a leader without leadership role
- Facilitator is an equal without leadership role

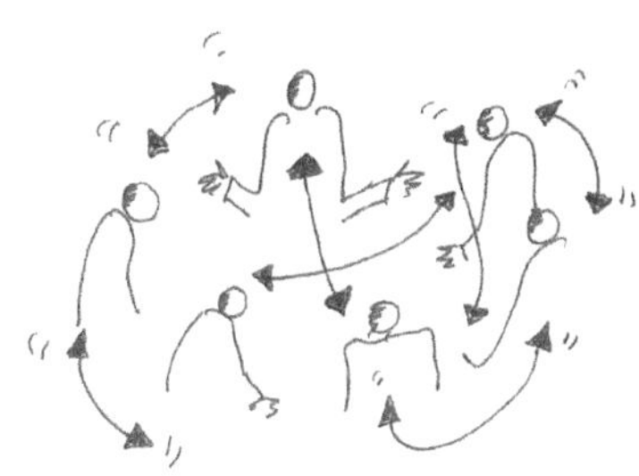

What makes a good facilitator?

Personal Qualities

- Humility
- Generosity
- Patience
- Understanding
- Acceptance
- Affirmation
- Perception
- Ability to challenge

Facilitation skills

- Listening to others
- Communicating clearly
- Checking understanding, summarising and drawing together different ideas
- Thinking and acting creatively
- Managing people's feelings
- Encouraging humour and respect
- Being well prepared whilst remaining flexible
- Keeping to time without being driven by it

Key facilitation skills: Listening Skills

Listening skills are vital for effective facilitation. It is very important to give your whole attention to someone and to be able to process and reflect on what they have just said. One way to develop our listening skills is to recognise our weaknesses in this area. The following scenarios below demonstrate bad listening habits. Look through them and recognise which habits you may have and consider how you might address them.

On-off listening

This arises from the fact that we think 4 times as fast as we can speak giving us spare thinking time for personal concerns etc. To overcome this, pay more attention to the non-verbal signs like gestures, hesitation etc to pick up the feeling level.

Red Flag Listening

To some people, certain words are like a red flag to a bull. When we hear them we get upset and stop listening.To overcome this barrier, find out which words affect us personally and try to listen attentively to someone more sympathetic to this issue.

Open ears closed mind listening

Sometimes we decide rather quickly that the subject or the speaker is boring or we jump to conclusions that we can predict what the speaker will say; and so we conclude that there is no reason to listen because we will hear nothing new if we do. It is much better to listen and find out whether this is true or not.

Glassy-eyed listening

Sometimes we look at the speaker but our minds are somewhere else and our dreamy expression gives us away. If you notice people looking glassy-eyed, suggest a break or change the pace.

Too-deep for me listening

When ideas are too complex and complicated, we should force ourselves to follow the discussion. Often, if we don't understand, others don't either, and it may help the group to ask for clarification or an example when possible.

Don't rock the boat listening

People do not like to have their favourite ideas, prejudices and points of view overturned. When that happens we may stop listening or become defensive. However if we listen we can understand the other viewpoint and respond constructively.

Listening to people helps them feel valued and affirms them for who they are.

"Wisdom is the reward you get for a lifetime of listening when you'd have preferred to talk."
Doug Larson

"Every person in this life has something to teach me—and as soon as I accept that, I open myself to truly listening."
Catherine Doucette

"The most basic of all human needs is the need to understand and be understood. The best way to understand people is to listen to them."
Ralph Nichol

Good listening is essential for asking the right questions which is a pre-requisite for building good relationships with a group and helping a group to achieve its task. It is also important to listen to what is not being said and what is being hidden under the surface.

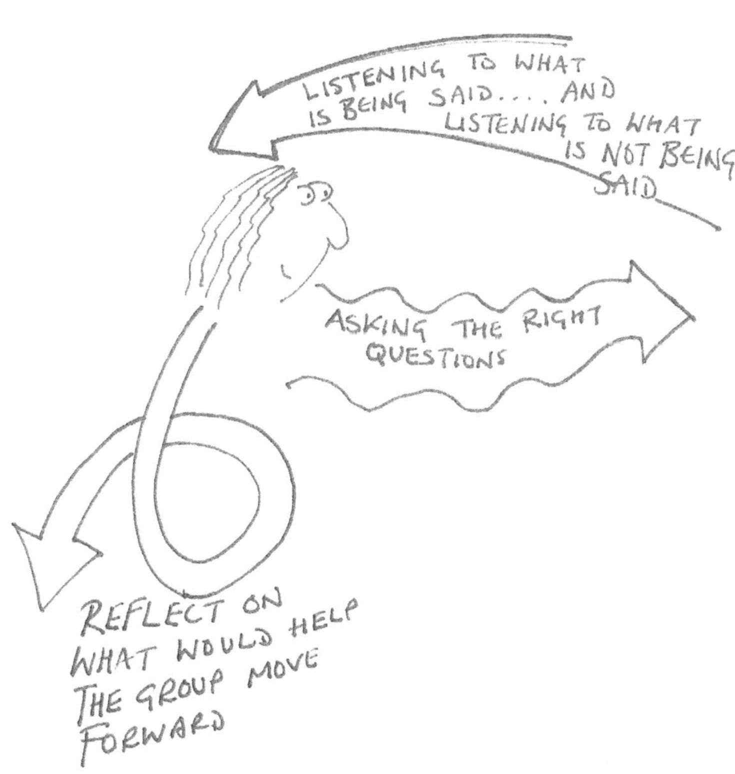

Asking the right questions

Asking open questions will enable you to get more information than closed questions which just require a yes or no answer.

This is especially true when you want to know what someone thinks about something.

The Hand method

A good way of remembering to ask open questions is to think of each finger on the hand as a different type of open question (see hand below).

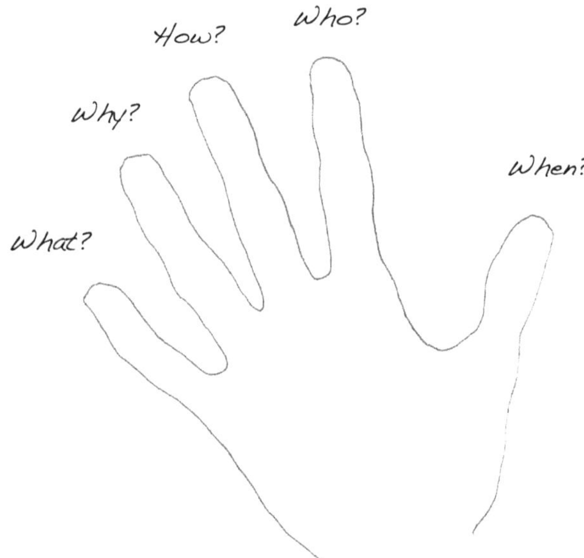

Questions for clarifying a problem

- I am not clear about...
- If you had to describe your challenge in five key words what would they be?
- Can you expand more on that point?
- Why has this come about?
- What caused it in the first place?
- I would like to explore further why...
- Are you saying that...
- Are the questions we are asking helpful at this stage?
- Can we try to summarise this challenge in a sentence?

Questions to help you move a group forward

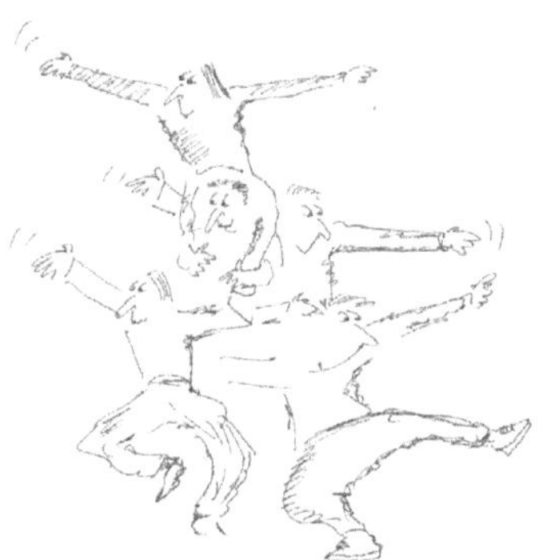

- What does this make you feel?
- Are you being honest with yourself about this situation?
- What worries you the most?
- What gives you most energy about this situation?
- What impact does this have on you and others?
- What would be the ideal solution for you if you had all the resources you needed?
- What options do you think we could use in the short-term?
- Which is the best option for you?
- What support would you need to take this forward?
- Have you thought of this idea?

Questions for making a decision and a plan of action

- Why do you think this is the best option?
- What is stopping you?
- What is the worst thing that could happen if you took this option?
- How do think you would feel after you have taken this action?
- Is this action realistic?
- What extra support might you need?

Giving helpful feedback

The giving and receiving of feedback involves using a set of skills which require very careful handling. It requires courage, tact, honesty, understanding and respect for ourselves and for others. When not done well, it can create defensiveness and tension; its effects can range from being meaningless to devastating. When done well, the effects can be enormously beneficial to individuals and those with whom they come into contact.

Guidelines for giving feedback

- Be descriptive and evaluative (what you saw and liked and disliked) but not judgmental (this was right or wrong)
- Be specific, not general
- Focus on visible behaviour, not invisible mental states such as attitudes, values and needs
- Be wary of making assumptions about the intentions of the person
- Report on feelings and impact of behaviour on you
- Time feedback appropriately
- Be positive, not negative. Emphasise what could be done differently
- Ensure feedback is about something that can be acted upon (e.g. not a nervous stammer)
- Be prepared to check the accuracy of your feedback
- Don't be personal/depersonalise it

Guidelines for receiving feedback

- Listen
- Check your understanding
- Try not to be defensive
- Remember the feedback is for your benefit
- Be willing to seek it to enhance your own performance
- Feel free to acknowledge the effort of the giver
- You choose what you will ultimately change about your behaviour, if anything

Summary

Facilitation is about:

- Empowering others
- Showing commitment to the value and potential of people
- Change that is far-reaching and sustainable, due to the building up of strong relationships, the quality of learning and because the group owns the process

"But with the best leaders,
When the work is done,
The task accomplished,
The people will say,
We have done this ourselves"

Lao Tzu 500 BC

The Adult Learning Cycle

The Role of the Facilitator

People learn best through having an experience which they can reflect on and draw conclusions from as to how they might act or behave differently in the future. Facilitation draws on the adult learning cycle as the main way of helping people learn. In facilitation, the direct experience comes through things such as a sketch or role play, an activity or task, or simply a brainstorm about a topic.

This is followed by an opportunity for participants to reflect on the experience, perhaps in small groups. This helps people to think about what they have experienced and what it might mean to them.

The next stage is the analysis of the experience which pools everybody's reflections into some principles or best practice which can be used in the future.

Application considers the practical steps needed to apply these principles into each participant's situation and identifies the barriers that need to be overcome so that the application can be effective.

"It is not the strongest of the species that survive, nor the most intelligent, but the ones most responsive to change"
Charles Darwin

"I am always doing that which I cannot do, in order that I may learn how to do it"
Pablo Picasso

1. Direct experience
2. Reflecting on experience
3. Analysis of experience
4. Application

The learning cycle can be applied across any time scale from one hour to a whole day. A common mistake when following the learning cycle is not to spend enough time thinking about the application and the barriers to helping people apply their learning back to the work place. As a guide, seek to use 20% of the time giving people a direct experience, another 20% on reflecting on the experience, 30% on analysing the experience and drawing principles and lessons from the experience, and a final 30% on thinking through the application and potential barriers to applying the learning.

Principles of Adult Learning

Adult learning occurs when:

1. It is self-directed - adults can share responsibility for their own learning because they know their own needs.
2. It fills an immediate need - motivation to learn is highest when it meets the immediate needs of the learner.
3. It is participative - participation in the learning process is active, not passive.
4. It is experiential - the most effective learning is from shared experience; learners learn from each other, and the trainer often learns from the learners.
5. It is reflective - maximum learning from a particular experience occurs when a person takes time to reflect back on it, draw conclusions, and derive principles for application to similar experiences in the future.
6. It provides feedback - effective learning requires feedback that is corrective but supportive.
7. It shows respect for the learner - mutual respect and trust between trainer and learner can help the learning process.
8. There is a safe atmosphere - A cheerful relaxed person learns more easily than one who is fearful, embarrassed or angry.

Comfort Stretch Panic

When facilitating a group, it's good to bear in mind the comfort-stretch-panic model. When you get people to move out of their comfort zone they learn more. However, it is important to know how far they can be stretched because if stretched too far, panic will occur and the learning is lost.

The more exposure to risk and challenge, the greater the learning. However, it is vital in the stretch phase to provide plenty of support and encouragement.

When facilitating, it is important to choose activities that will produce an appropriate stretch.

SECTION TWO

BRINGING THE GROUP TOGETHER

Bringing the group together

When a new group gets together there can be a sense of uncertainty and anxiety for a number of reasons. The members of the group do not know each other and may have varying experiences of the topic. People may have different motivations for being on the course and all of these present challenges for bringing a group together.

The activities that you choose to do when a group first gets together should be aimed at:

- helping the group feel safe and relaxed
- creating a sense of belonging and common purpose
- creating a sense of fun
- warming your group up to the topic
- establishing hopes and fears

Introductory activities

Listed below are a range of introductory activities which need to be selected according to the size and nature of the group you are working with. Some of these activities could be combined to enrich the introductory process.

Talking in pairs

In this exercise, the group is divided into pairs and they interview each other using a simple set of questions which are written up on a flipchart. The questions could include:

- What is their name?
- What is one thing they like about where they live?
- What are their hopes for the course?

Each pair feedback to the wider group by sharing the answers that their partner has given.

Market place

This is very good for large groups where there is not enough time for every individual to introduce themselves to the whole group. In this exercise, you invite everyone to stand up and go and find someone they haven't spoken to yet and ask them a question such as:

How was their journey to this training event?

The facilitator then interviews a few pairs to get a flavour of the answers, then sets another question such as

What is one thing you value about your organisation?

The group then find another person to talk to about this question, and the facilitator again interviews a few pairs, and then sets a last question such as:

What do you most hope to gain from this course?

This is debriefed in a similar way to the above.

This activity creates a good buzz in the room and allows everyone to say something to someone at the start of the course which helps the more shy or reserved members of the group to engage.

Matches

Again, this a good activity to use with a large group. Write a few introductory questions on a flipchart and then go round the group with a box of matches. Each person must strike a match and answer the questions in the time that the match burns. Questions could include:

- What is your name?
- What is your organisation?
- What is one thing you like about your organisation?
- What is your favourite food?
- What is your favourite film and why?

The beauty of this exercise is that it means every one has to be very concise and there is no opportunity for one person to talk at length. It also creates a light atmosphere as the flame burns down the match.

Obviously it is important to establish where the smoke alarms are in the room and whether anyone has any objection to striking a match. If so, the facilitator should strike the match for them. This game can also be used at other points in the group work such as reviewing the day or managing feedback from a particular activity.

North South East West

This is a good activity for energising as well as introducing the group to each other. You start off by standing in the middle of the room and saying that you represent where the group is now geographically. For example, "I am the centre of London". You then point out where in the room north, south, east and west are and ask the group to stand where they were born in relation to you. Once they have taken their positions, you ask them where they were born and one thing they like about their organisation.

Then ask them to move to where they live now and what they hope to gain from the course or groupwork. Finally ask them to move again to where they would like to live in the future if money was no object and ask them how they would like to use the learning from the course back in their own work.

Variations of this activity: Disaster awareness

When you have asked the group to stand where they were born you then explain you are going to look at varying degrees of disaster risk. If there is a high risk, they stand up, if it is a medium risk they squat and if it is a low risk, they sit on the floor. Then ask them what risk is there of

flooding
drought
drug abuse
windstorms
hurricanes
civil conflict

With each of these, the group will create a visual graph of the risks represented in their area, country or region. This makes for a good introduction to any training on disaster management or social risk.

Knowing your community

Another way of using North South East West is for a local community to go through a series of questions about their community so as to build a common understanding of the issues in the local area. First of all, begin by asking where people live and what they like about their community. Then ask them to move to areas they think are good in the community that they would want to celebrate. Then ask them to move to areas which are of concern and need addressing.

This is a good way of mapping the community and getting the group to establish a common understanding of issues through moving around the room and creating discussion groups in the areas where people are standing.

Tools for introducing topics

Brown Bags

This tool has many benefits for engaging groups at a variety of levels and is an excellent way of introducing a subject. The key steps are:

1. Decide what questions you want to ask and then write these on A4 pieces of card.
2. Stick the questions around the walls of the room.
3. Underneath each question stick a brown bag or envelope with masking tape on the wall along with some post-it notes.
4. As the participants arrive, ask them to go round the room answering the questions on the post-it notes and then put their answers in the brown bags or envelopes. If it is a large group, ask them to walk round in pairs.
5. Once everyone has done this, divide the group into small groups and give each group one or two bags to analyse, grouping the answers into common themes.
6. Each group should then feedback to the large group.

Examples of questions

If you are running a course on facilitation skills you could use these questions:

- What is facilitation?
- What is the difference between facilitation and teaching?
- When would you use facilitation?
- What are some of the challenges of facilitating groups?
- If your organisation was a form of transport what would it be?

If you are running a course on monitoring and evaluation, you could use these questions:

- What is monitoring?
- What is evaluation?
- Why is monitoring and evaluation important?
- What is a qualitative indicator?
- What is a quantitative indicator?
- What are your hopes and fears about being on this course?

This activity gets a group engaged and talking straight away and you avoid that awkward stage at the beginning of the course when people are unsure of what to do or who to speak to. It also has the effect of gaining a lot of information in a short period of time. It helps the facilitator know what level of knowledge and experience there is in the room, while at the same time the anonimity of the exercise helps to maintain the safety aspect.

The brown bags exercise as a demonstration of good learning

This exercise is very good for deepening individuals own learning as the process of using the brown bags goes through three cycles of learning.

The first cycle is when the individual reflects on each question and places their answer on a post-it to go in the bag.

The second cycle is when the group is divided into smaller groups to process the bags and to look at the common themes for each answer. Here the learning is in seeing what other people have written and gaining insights from that as well as analysing the information into common themes.

The third cycle is when the whole group comes together in a plenary session and each small group shares their responses to each question. The discussion that follows each presentation creates another cycle of learning as the whole group learns new insights together. At this point, the facilitator can add their own reflections and questions to deepen the learning further.

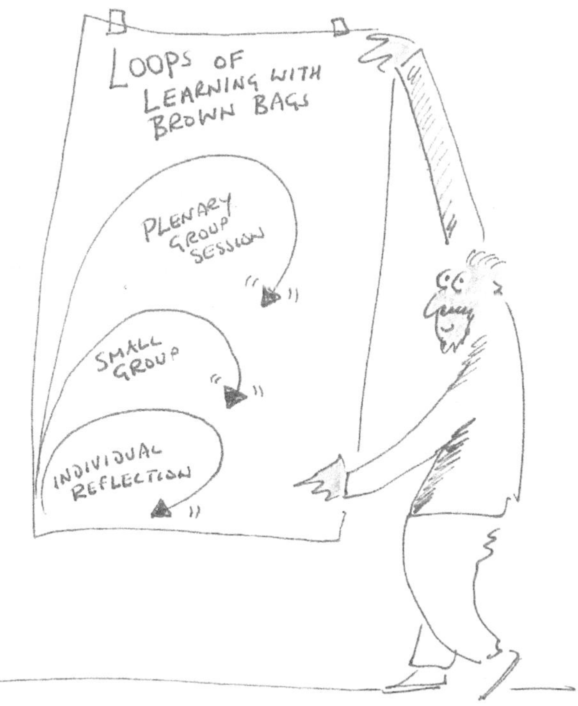

Spectrum Lines

This is a good way of finding out how your participants feel about certain aspects of the topic you are exploring. The steps of this exercise are as follows:

1. Create two A4 cards, one saying Strongly Agree and one saying Strongly Disagree. Make the cards interesting by adding a picture, maybe a happy face on strongly agree and an unhappy face on strongly disagree.
2. Stick these cards on opposite walls in the room
3. Have a list of statements to do with the topic you are covering in the course and ask the participants to stand along an imaginary line from strongly agree to strongly disagree according to how they feel about each statement. Include some light hearted statements to introduce an element of fun.
4. After each question ask a few participants why they are standing where they are. If it is a large group you can ask them to discuss together in small groups.
5. After some of the feedback has been given you could ask if anyone wants to move from where they are standing.
6. Alternatively you could ask someone standing at one extreme to say what they think the person standing at the other extreme is going to say. This is a good way of getting people to put themselves in other peoples shoes.

Some examples of statements

- Men are better drivers than women
- Men are better cooks than women
- It's too late to do anything about climate change
- The main cause of youth crime is bad parenting
- People only change in a crisis
- I'd rather lose an arm than a leg

SECTION THREE

GENERATING IDEAS AND PLANNING

Generating ideas and planning

This section looks at some simple tools that help groups generate ideas and plan in a way that involves everybody so that there is shared ownership and understanding of what the group is trying to do. Some common problems in planning are:

- Groups are consulted but then someone else goes away and writes it all up in a way that nobody really understands or owns.

- Often groups are involved in brainstorms to get ideas flowing but these can become overwhelming and confusing and sometimes strong individuals can dominate the final decision.
- Often brainstorming is very limited by being contained on one big sheet of paper, and the ideas often get stuck or don't give synergy to new ideas.

The challenge of coming up with a new idea

One of the challenges of coming up with a new idea is that sometimes the ideas are not creative enough and the way brainstorming is done is very limiting. In addition, in the process of brainstorming there is often a point, which can be termed as the groan zone, where the group runs out of energy because it struggles to consolidate the ideas and people start to feel frustrated and give up. This is summarised in the diagram below.

The challenges therefore, are to make the brainstorming as creative as possible, to manage the group through the groan zone, and to help them prioritise and support the best ideas.

The following tools help to address some of the challenges highlighted above.

Ranking

Ranking is a really good way of involving a group and getting everyone's contribution. A wide range of ideas and options are explored using coloured cards and these are grouped into themes and then prioritised based on certain criteria chosen by the group.

Step-by-step guide:

1. First define the area you want to get ideas for, such as the vision for your community for the next ten years, or a problem that is relevant to the people in your group.
2. Divide into groups and ask the groups to brainstorm on to coloured cards any ideas they have - they should be as creative as possible, and even unrealistic. This helps the group to think outside the box. At this stage, the group should not be thinking of practicalities.
3. Each group then in turn sticks their ideas up on the wall explaining them to the other groups as they do so.
4. Ask two or three people then to group these ideas into themes.
5. This is a great way of ensuring that any plans that are put in place as a result of this ranking technique has the ownership of the group.

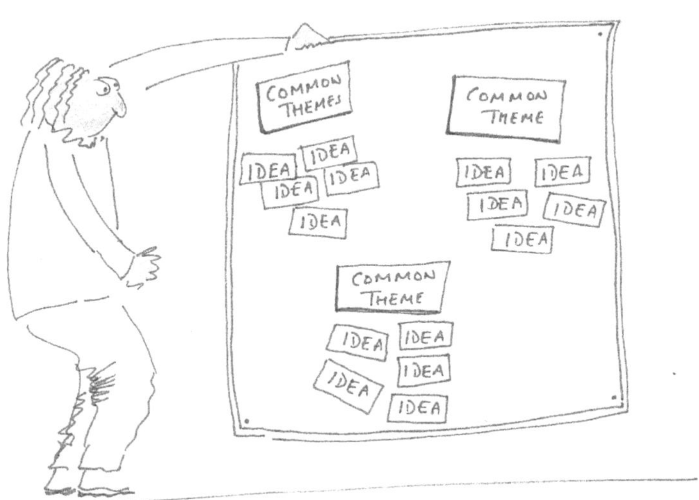

6. Then, as a large group, decide the criteria you are going to use to prioritise these ideas; for example, they must be environmentally friendly, within a certain budget, using their own resources.

7. Having decided the criteria, then discard any ideas that do not fit with the chosen criteria.
8. Of the ideas that remain, ask the whole group to vote on which ideas they prefer. They could have five votes each and distribute these votes how they like; for example, they could put one vote on five ideas or all five on one.
9. When everyone has voted, list the top three ideas. You could use the swimming pool technique on the following page to find out the level of commitment to each of the three ideas.
10. Alternatively you could group the top ideas according to when they could be achieved. This helps the group think practically about the resources they have, and what they can do by when.

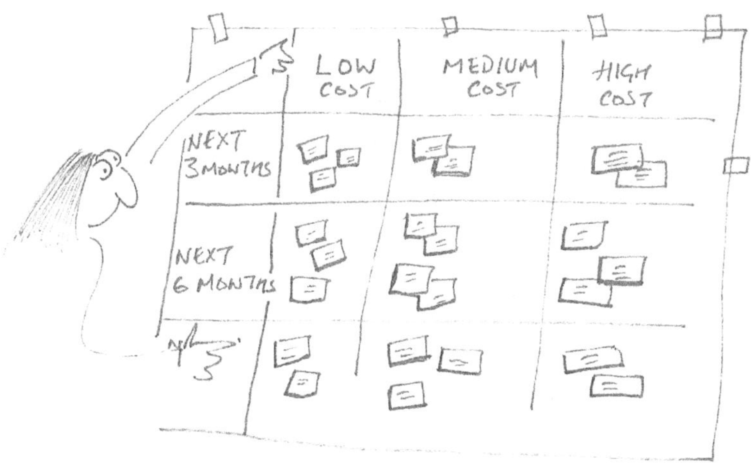

Swimming Pool

This is a great way of finding out how committed everyone is to an idea, a project or an initiative. Make up cards to represent the different areas at a public swimming pool as stated below. Place the cards around the room in the order shown. Then ask people to stand where they feel they are in relation to their commitment to an idea or initiative. This can be done early on in the process and then later on when the initiative is in full swing.

To make the cards, use simple drawings or print suitable images from the internet and then laminate the cards.

Car park - not at all committed - not interested

Reception - maybe have a look at it - but not paid yet - could still go back

Changing rooms - paid your money and willing to have a go

Toddler pool - testing it out but not going to get too involved

Shallow End - maybe slightly more committed - with potential to go deeper

Deep End - very committed

Diving Board - committed and prepared to take a few risks

Flume - committed and excited about being involved

Once everyone has stood next to a card, ask people for their reasons for standing there. Then see if any others have changed their mind as a result of what has been said. Explore people's fears. For instance if someone is standing at reception, ask them what would it take for them to get into the changing room.

This is a good exercise because everyone gets to express a view, and a mixture of enthusiasm, fears and practicalities can lead to some rich discussions on what needs to happen to make something work.

For international workers, you could adapt this for your own context. Instead of using a swimming pool you could use all the stages involved in going to the market by bus.

Once you have come up with the top ideas using ranking, and tested the commitment of the group to each idea, you can then turn them into practical action plans, using the minibus method on the next page.

The Minibus exercise

Purpose

This exercise helps the group plan a project in a way that everybody can understand and remember. If possible, try to get someone to draw a bus on a large piece of paper, similar to the picture below and display it somewhere where everyone can see it. Then discuss the questions that surround it. Use post-it notes to write ideas on each part of the minibus. This creates ownership for any plan that emerges from the discussions and also helps the group to think about the risks involved so they can take measures to address potential problems before they happen.

Tips for planning

1. Be clear about the problem you are seeking to address.
2. Check that the group you are working with have sufficient skills, experience and knowledge to undertake this particular project they have chosen. If they do not, then discuss where they could get additional help.
3. When using the minibus exercise, invite everybody to contribute to answering the different questions.
4. If the group is very big, then break it into smaller groups of four to five people to discuss the questions. If there are a lot of answers for each question, ask the group to prioritise the most important answers.

World Café - The Art of Conversation

World café is a good technique for generating and exploring ideas and is excellent for large groups.

The World Café approach is based upon enabling lots of people to have a number of conversations all at the same time but in a way that allows important questions and issues to be explored and recorded and used in the future. It is commonly used with groups of 50 - 100 people and has an informal café type atmosphere which allows participants to move freely to discuss questions and issues that are important to them.

The seven principles of the World Café are:

- Be clear about the purpose and context of the café for all the participants
- Create a friendly and hospitable environment
- Explore questions that are important
- Encourage everyone's contribution
- Encourage the sharing of ideas between different groups and individuals
- Look at patterns and common themes which can be explored in more depth later on
- Have fun - enjoy yourself

Methodology

The environment is set up like a café, with tables for four people, covered with paper tablecloths, flowers, some coloured pens and, if possible, candles, quiet music and refreshments. People sit four to a table and have a series of conversational rounds lasting from 20-45 minutes about one or more questions which are personally meaningful to them. At the end of each round, one person remains at each table as host, while each of the other three travel to separate tables.

Table hosts welcome newcomers to their tables and share the essence of the table's conversation so far. The newcomers relate any conversational threads which they are carrying and then the conversation continues, deepening as the round progresses. At the end of the second round, participants return to their original table or move on to other tables for one or more additional rounds, depending on the design of the café. In subsequent rounds they may explore a new question or go deeper into the original one. After three or more rounds, the whole group gathers to share and explore emerging themes, insights and learning, which are captured on flipcharts so that everyone can reflect on what is emerging in the room. At this point the Café may end or a further round may begin. In World Café, finding the right questions is a fundamental art and skill.

Questions like

> "What's important to you about this situation, and why do you care?" and "What are we not seeing (or talking about) that is vital to our progress?"

can open up new possibilities and energy. If you (as host) don't know what questions are right for a particular Café, you could ask as a first round question,

> "What question if answered, could make the greatest difference to the future of the situation we are exploring here?"

Mosaic Creative has used World Café with a number of International Aid Agencies.

SECTION FOUR

HOW TO FACILITATE ENERGISERS AND LEARNING GAMES

How to use energisers

Energisers are important for helping a group get to know each other and to create an atmosphere of fun and togetherness. They can also be used to break up any periods of long discussion and sitting around.

Examples of energisers

Talking in pairs

Purpose:

To help people to get to know one another

Time: 10 - 15 mins

Step-by-step guide:

1. Ask the group to get into pairs and talk for two minutes to each other about their journey here today.
2. Then ask the group to find a different partner and talk about one thing they value about their children.
3. Finally, mix up the pairs again and ask them to talk about what they hope the group will achieve in working together.
4. After each two minute conversation ask for some feedback from one or two pairs. It might be a good idea to note down the comments from the last question as it will be good to see if these expectations are achieved after the group has been working together for a while.
5. Feel free to use your own questions instead of the ones above to suit the group.

Symbolic Introductions

Purpose:

To introduce the participants to each other and create a sense of belonging

Materials:

Objects lying around, in or near the room

Time: 20 - 30 minutes depending on the size of the group

Step-by-step guide:

1. Ask the participants to form groups of three and find an object, perhaps outside, that they feel symbolises their village or street.
2. Ask them to introduce themselves and explain why they chose this object as their symbol.

Comments:

This exercise is useful for encouraging participants to open up and share feelings early in the workshop. Introductions are made while searching for and agreeing on a symbol. If you are not familiar with the region, hearing about the symbols is a good introduction to the local value system.

Fruit Salad

Purpose:

To energise the group and to form sub-groups for further group work

Materials:

Chairs arranged in a circle, one for each participant

Time: 10 mins

Step-by-step guide:

1. Ask participants to sit in the chairs with the trainer standing in the middle, and explain that this is an energiser that will require very active participation.
2. Let the participants name as many fruits as you need sub-groups. Ask one person to choose a fruit, their neighbour another fruit and so on until the required number of fruit is reached. The next person in the circle takes the name of the first fruit and so on until everyone, including the trainer, has a fruit name.
3. The trainer in the middle calls out the name of one fruit. All those people who are that fruit must change chairs. The trainer must also try to sit down and should succeed as they have half the distance to travel.
4. One person will be left in the middle who then repeats the process by calling out another fruit. When 'fruit salad' is called out, everyone must change chairs.

Comments:

1. This exercise can be a great deal of fun and all participants will be fully active in the chaos. As the trainer you should conclude by allowing yourself to be left in the middle.
2. The fruit names can then be used as groups for further group work.
3. This game mixes heirarchies and relaxes participants. It also divides friends and colleagues into separate groups as they tend to sit together in the circle.
4. There are endless variations to this game, including, 'Jungle' 'Zoo' (animals), 'vegetable soup' 'meat stew' (vegetables or meat), cocktail (drinks) and rainbow (colours).

Breakthrough

Purpose:

To energise the group and illustrate the importance of coordination and communication

Time: 15 minutes

Step-by-step guide:

1. Divide the participants into two groups of equal numbers and have them stand in two lines holding hands facing each other (about two metres apart).
2. Group A is asked to break through group B. No one is allowed to talk.
3. When the breakthrough occurs, the two groups are told they have five to ten minutes to plan a second breakthrough or defence.
4. Repeat the attempt.

Comments:

Ask the participants to reflect on the difference between the two breakthroughs. The first breakthrough usually occurs fairly early. The second is more difficult.

Ask the group to reflect on the importance of coordination and communication, and what can be achieved as a group compared to a set of individuals.

Group Sculpture

Purpose:

To illustrate, in a non-threatening manner, the interaction between group members on an individual issue or general subject

Time: 15 - 30 minutes

Step-by-step guide:

Divide the participants into groups, and ask them to create a human sculpture that best reflects an issue that is appropriate to the training at the time. For example, they could create sculptures of things they like about their community or challenges in the community.

Comments:

This is an energetic activity that causes a lot of laughter but also tests people's creativity to produce a sculpture to reflect an issue that everyone can identify with. An interesting version of this is to get groups to sculpture a form of transport that reflects an aspect of community life. For example, a bus can represent a community working together.

How to facilitate learning games

Sometimes people learn best through practical activities and taking time to reflect on what happened in the activity. In this section we explore a number of learning games which enable participants to reflect on a specific issue. The value of learning games is that they encourage whole group participation, provide energy to the group and can provoke lively discussions.

Tips for learning games

Some key tips for facilitating a learning game are as follows:

- Practice the learning game yourself with a group of friends before you do it with others.
- Explain clearly how the learning activity is to be done and in what order. Before they start, check everyone understands how it is to be done.
- When the activity is over, make sure you debrief it in a way that is similar to the learning cycle.
  - what did they feel during the exercise?
  - what do they think the exercise illustrates in regard to their daily lives?
  - what does this activity tell us about how we should behave and act in the future?

Examples of learning games

The knotty problem

Purpose:

To demonstrate to participants that groups empowered to solve their own problems are much more successful than if instructed by outsiders.

Time: 10 - 15 minutes

Step-by-step guide:

1. Select one or two participants to act as managers. They are asked to leave the room while you instruct the rest of the group.
2. Ask the remaining participants to hold hands in a circle and tie themselves up into as entangled a knot as possible. They must not let go of each other's hands.
3. Once the knot is complete, the managers are asked to return and unravel the knot within 3 minutes, using verbal instructions only.
4. The first attempt is generally not successful and sometimes produces an even more complex knot. Now repeat the exercise with the managers participating in the knot. When the knot is ready, simply ask the participants to get out of the knot themselves. The second untying process is usually much quicker.

Comments:

Ask the participants to comment on what relevance this has to the real world using these questions:

1. What does the game tell us about the role of outsiders/managers and insiders (in the knot)?
2. What does the exercise tell us about the effectiveness of 'outsiders' and 'managers' in organising people?
3. What are the lessons to be learned for facilitating a group involved in problem solving?

Rope Square

Purpose:

To explore how a group works together on a difficult task. To illustrate how people adopt different roles in a group.

Materials:

A piece of rope that is tied so that it forms a circle, sufficiently long so that half the total group can hold on to it with both hands.

Time: 20 - 30 minutes

Step-by-step guide:

1. Divide the group into 2 - the silent observers and the square formers.
2. Lay the rope in a circle on the floor in the middle of the room.
3. Ask the square forming group to stand in a circle around the rope. The observers watch in silence.
4. Ask the square forming group to pick up the rope with both hands, then close their eyes and walk around in a circle a couple of times to disorient themselves. Alternatively, you could use blindfolds.
5. Then ask the group to form a perfect square with the rope (without looking).
6. The other group should observe the dynamics without commenting.
7. Change the roles of the group and then debrief.

Comments:

This is a potentially very powerful exercise, revealing a lot about different types of group members, including leaders, followers, people who disrupt the group etc. There are always too many leaders. Use the discussion to draw these points out:

- Who felt frustrated?
- Were the instructions given by other group members clear?
- How did you respond to contradictory orders or requests?
- Who took the lead? Why? When?
- Who played a bridging role?
- Who kept quiet?
- Who cross-checked and evaluated orders from others?

The intention is not to make the evaluation personal but to point out the range of qualities of group members and how they interact successfully and unsuccessfully in completing a task.

Toxic Waste

Purpose:

Practical teamwork task to see how members work together.

Time: 45 minutes

Materials:

- String to mark out an area 3m square
- 3 x 4m length of rope
- A large plastic bottle filled with water (3 - 5l)
- A range of objects to distract group from the task – brooms, dustbin etc.

Step-by-step guide:

1. Mark out a square measuring 3m x 3m and place the bottle full of water in the middle.
2. Explain to the group that they have to rescue the bottle only using the materials provided. They must not reach over into the square or they will be burned by the toxic gases. The bottle must be lifted directly up and away from the square and must not be dragged or pulled across the ground.
3. Divide the group into 2 teams and give each team 2 mins to plan how they might achieve this task.
4. Each group takes it in turns to attempt to achieve the task.
5. Once they have achieved the task, debrief and review. Key areas could include involvement of everyone in decision making and sharing ideas, identifying skills and experiences, organising roles and contributions.

Trainer's tip

The bottle can be removed by running two parallel ropes either side of the bottle, then gently twisting each end of the parallel ropes together so that they tighten round the body of the bottle. This will take a few minutes until the bottle is caught in a tight grip of the twisted ropes. It can then be lifted easily and smoothly off the ground.

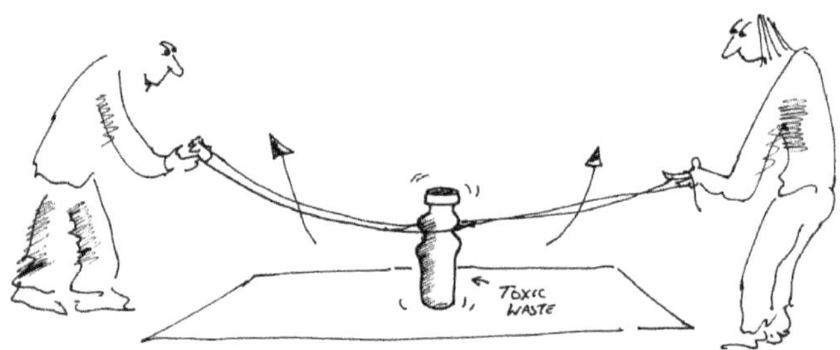

Lowering the stick

Purpose:

This is a good game for getting people to think about the challenges of working together.

Step-by-step guide:

1. Divide the group into two lines of up to eight people.
2. Place a long stick or bamboo between the two lines and get each person to hold it with one finger.
3. Make sure that the stick is level and everyone is holding it and then tell the group that they have to lower it together making sure the stick is level, until it reaches the ground.
4. Discuss with the group what helped the task be achieved and what were the challenges.
5. What can we learn from this for how we should work together.

Learning points to discuss with the group are:

- Achieving a task always requires an element of leadership and co-ordination
- Doing your own thing regardless of others upsets the equilibrium
- When you are involved in a project there is more than one goal – to achieve the task and keep everyone together and involved
- We need to keep everyone together and involved to have a real sense of achievement

You may know of other energisers that would be equally good for getting people to think about working together, so feel free to use those instead.

Making the Longest Line

Purpose:

This is a good activity for getting a group to think about what they can do with their own resources. It can generate a lot of fun and laughter as well as provide some useful learning. In using this exercise it is important to be sensitive to local culture and tradition.

Step-by-step guide:

1. Ask the group to form two lines with an equal number of people in each line.
2. Explain they are going to use anything they have on them to make the longest possible line.
3. Each person must be in contact with another person either by means of a part of the body or an article of clothing.
4. The team that wins is the one that forms the longest line.

Questions

1. To what lengths were people prepared to go to make the line as long as possible?
2. What were the barriers to people sharing what they had?
3. What does this exercise teach us about using our own resources?

Learning points to discuss with the group are:

- It can surprise us when we see what we can achieve only using what we have.
- Sometimes challenging situations produce natural leaders.
- Once people have a clear vision of what is needed they become motivated and energised.
- Challenging situations can produce creativity. For example, people may decide to lie down on the ground to make the line longer or find creative uses for their clothes and accessories.
- For some people this exercise may be uncomfortable and sometimes, giving up our resources for the common good, can be challenging and uncomfortable too.

Facilitating group discussion

Flies on the wall activity

Start this activity with a brainstorm of "what makes a good facilitator?" Write all the ideas up so that everybody can see them. Explain that the group will practise these skills in the activity. Explain that each person will take turns to facilitate a discussion on a topic chosen by the group.

Divide the group into two, one smaller than the other and invite the smaller group to form a circle inside the other group. Assign a facilitator for ten to fifteen minutes and ask them to lead the discussion. The outer circle are to feedback on what they thought went well and what could be improved. Then invite the next person to facilitate the same topic or a new topic. If there is time, form a new group from the outer circle of participants.

Facilitation dilemmas activity

Split the group into smaller groups of five or six people. Ask each group in turn to do a role play of one of the following situations. The rest of the group should then discuss how they could deal with that situation.

- Discussions are being dominated by one or two people
- Some people are not contributing at all to a discussion
- A discussion is losing its focus and going off at a tangent

SECTION FIVE

REVIEWING GROUP WORK AND TASKS

Reviewing group work and tasks

In many situations it is useful to have tools that can help review either how well a group is working together or how a project or initiative is going. In this section there are a selection of tools to help a facilitator conduct a simple review.

Reviewing tools

The Traffic Light

This is a good tool for reviewing how a group is working together.

Draw a traffic light on a flipchart. Then think of your team in terms of behaviours and write by the appropriate coloured light some things the team could consider:

Red - things we could stop doing because they are not helpful to the organisation

Yellow - things we could start doing because they would help the organisation

Green - things we could continue doing because they are benefiting the organisation

Team Process review

This is a good exercise to do after a specific event or activity. When the event is over, get the group together and ask:

1. What did your team do that helped the completion of the task?
2. What things hindered the completion of the task?
3. What would you do differently?
4. What did you learn about team effectiveness?

Hats and scarves

This is a good activity to do at the end of a workshop day to find out what the group has learned and is taking away from the sessions. Collect together a selection of hats and scarves which are quite diverse and ask all the participants to choose one that they think best represents the learning or insights they have gained. Then ask each person to share why they have selected their hat or scarf.

Alternatively this exercise can be used for getting a person's opinion of the project they have been involved in as part of evaluating it.

Using objects to express opinions

In our experience of working with vulnerable and marginalised groups, using objects such as hats or even a fluffy toy chicken can help shy individuals find the confidence to speak to the whole group. This is because the focus is on the object, not the person, and this feels less threatening to them.

Pipe cleaners

This is similar to hats and scarves, except this time, you give each participant a pipe cleaner and you invite them to make it into the shape of something they think they have learned from the course or by working together with the group. Once they have done this, they share it with the group and you can stick them on a large piece of flipchart paper with sellotape. This can be quite challenging but good for getting people to think laterally and creatively.

The Evaluation Wheel

The evaluation wheel is made up of a series of ever increasing circles drawn on to a large piece of paper and numbered from one to ten. The wheel is then divided into segments to look a bit like a dartboard as shown in the picture below. Each segment of the dartboard represents an area of the course, such as presentations, group working and logistics. The facilitator invites participants to come and use a marker pen to mark on the dartboard the score they think each area deserves according to their experience of attending the course. This is a good method because it visualises the scores and helps the facilitator to gain a quick impression of what the participants are finding helpful and not helpful.

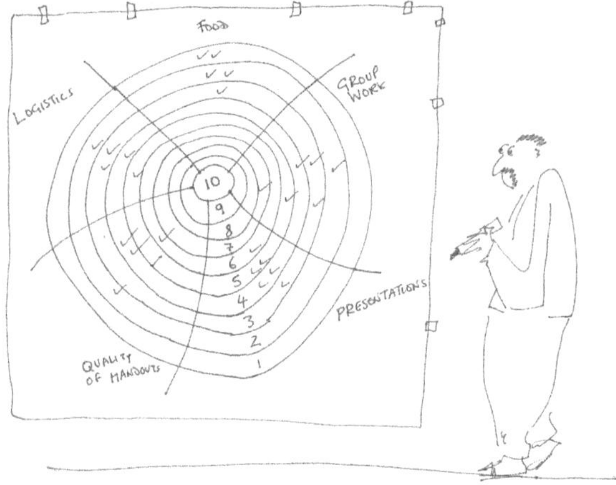

Big Brother Webcam

Another way of gathering stories is to use the Big Brother method where a laptop is set up with a webcam in a secluded space and participants can talk to the camera about what they feel about the course, an event or an activity. Clips from these video segments can be reviewed to identify key themes.

The Timeline

Purpose:

The purpose of this tool is to review a project from its beginning to the present time and to record the high and low points and achievements. It takes about one hour to complete.

Materials:

Large sheets of paper stuck together as one long sheet, and marker pens.

Step-by-step guide:

1. Roll the paper out on to tables or on the floor and explain that one end of the paper represents the beginning of the project.
2. The group draws a line from this point up to the present day. In doing this, they need to mark on the key events, both positive and negative of that period.
3. Encourage the group to draw or stick on pictures to symbolise the positive and negative experiences.
4. When the line is complete, encourage the group to discuss what contributed to the positive and negative experiences. Ask them to explore what they have learned and what they would do differently in the next project.

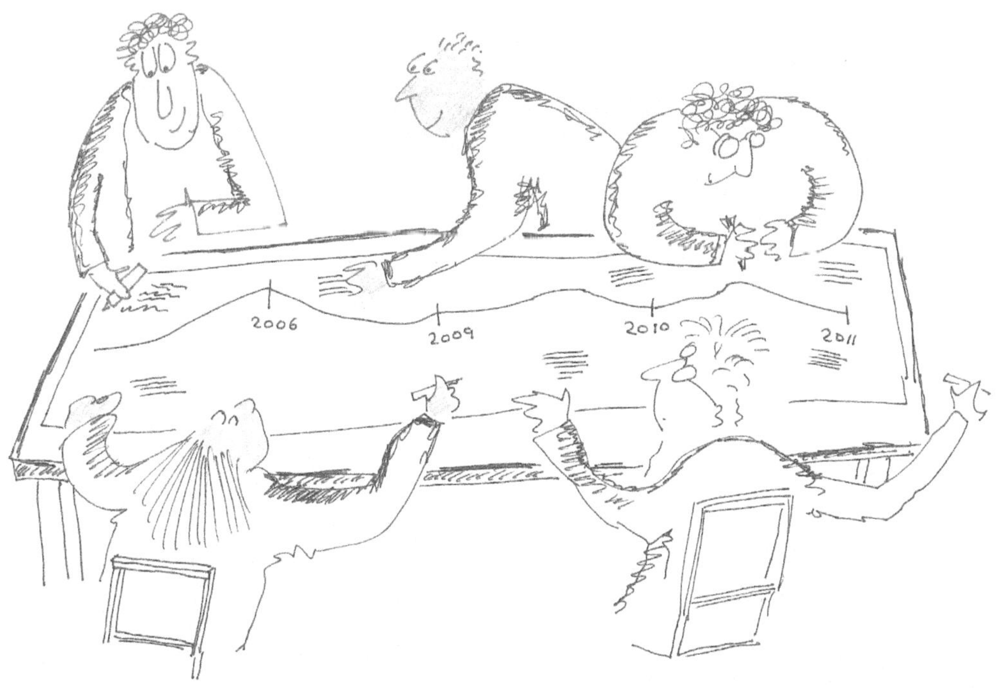

SECTION SIX

UNDERSTANDING GROUP DYNAMICS

Understanding group dynamics

A key quality of a good facilitator is to understand the dynamics of a group and how to respond appropriately to the different changes they go through. The facilitator needs to have one eye on the task that needs to be achieved and the other eye on what is happening in the group, in terms of individual and collective needs. It is not always easy to anticipate difficult moments or responses in the group and you can only learn how to deal with them through practice. However, it is always good to have a few ideas and tools up your sleeve for when things become tricky or heavy going.

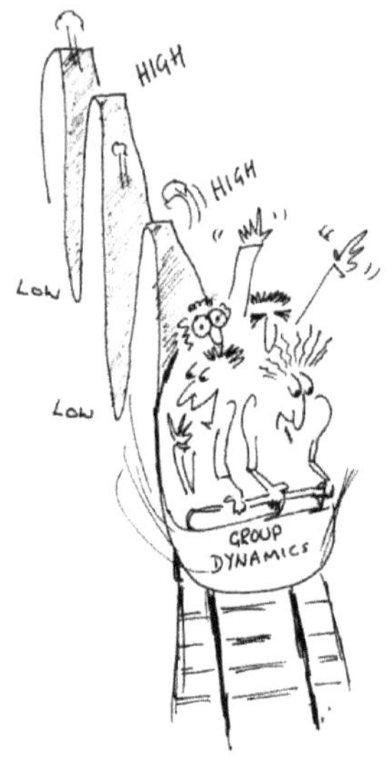

Another important aspect to bear in mind is to monitor the energy of the group and to be ready to make a change in the method or pace of the discussions.

"A good facilitator is a magician, who is ready to pull something out of the hat when things go wrong; he's a comedian who can laugh at himself and learn from his mistakes and he's a fanatic who is passionate about helping people to learn"
Anon

Understanding your group

Any new group will always have some fears and questions about how the experience is going to be. The job of a facilitator is to understand these fears and find ways of addressing them. The following questions and concerns describe some of the typical feelings people may have.

- Will I be accepted or rejected here?
- What exactly will these sessions be like?
- What risks will I have to take?
- How am I like other people here?
- How am I different from other people here?
- Will I feel pressured and pushed to perform in some way?
- How important will I be?
- Who will be the real leaders here?
- What can be achieved here?

What are their concerns and fears?

1. I'm afraid I'll look stupid
2. Will I tell too much about myself?
3. Will others like me?
4. What if they find out what I'm really like?
5. What if everyone rejects me?
6. I'm afraid I'll be withdrawn and passive
7. What will happen if I really open up my feelings?
8. Will I embarrass myself?
9. What if I'm asked to do something I don't want to do?
10. What if others can tell I'm afraid and nervous?

Ground rules

Ground rules are useful for making sure group behaviours stay positive and constructive. However, some group members may feel that ground rules are unnecessary and tedious.

A good way of making sure that ground rules are followed is by getting the group to select the rules themselves so there is ownership of them. Then agree on a reward of some kind for keeping the rules, such as a box of chocolates or a bottle of wine.

To make this successful, you will need to appoint someone who is going to monitor the ground rules and ensure that they are kept so that the group can enjoy the reward.

Some examples of ground rules:

- Everyone must turn up to the sessions on time
- Mobile phones must be turned off
- All contributions will be listened to and valued
- No interrupting
- Mutual respect etc

Tuckman's forming storming norming performing model

A key response to coping with the changing dynamic of a group is to get the group itself to recognise that it is going through a change and to help it think through how it might manage itself. It is often useful to point out the model below of Forming, Storming, Norming, Performing. This helps to create self awareness and understanding of how it is normal for groups to go through change.

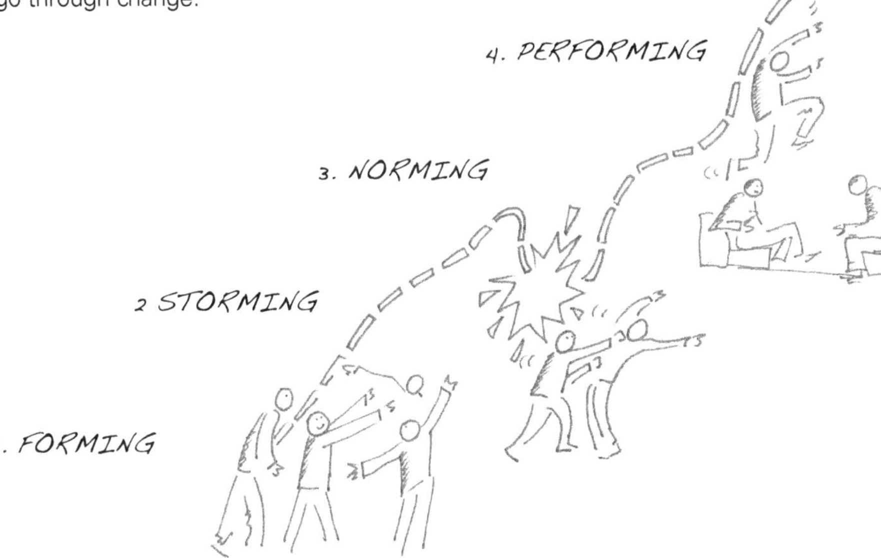

1. Forming

High dependence on leader for guidance and direction. Individual roles and responsibilities unclear. Leader must be prepared to answer lots of questions about the team's purpose, objectives and external relationships. Processes are often ignored. Leader directs.

2. Storming

Decisions don't come easily within the group. Team members vie for position. Clarity of purpose increases but plenty of uncertainties persist. Cliques and factions form. Team needs to be focused on goals to avoid being distracted by relationships and emotional issues. Leader coaches.

3. Norming

Agreement and consensus among team who respond well to facilitation by leader. Roles and responsibilities are clear and accepted. Big decisions are made by group agreement. Commitment and unity are strong. The team discusses and develops its processes and working style. Respect for the leader and some leadership is shared by the team. Leader facilitates and enables.

4. Performing

The team is more strategically aware. The team is clear about its purpose. The team has a shared vision and is able to stand on its own feet with no interference or participation from the leader. Disagreements occur but they are resolved positively. Leader stands back and provides a supportive role when needed.

The Power Continuum

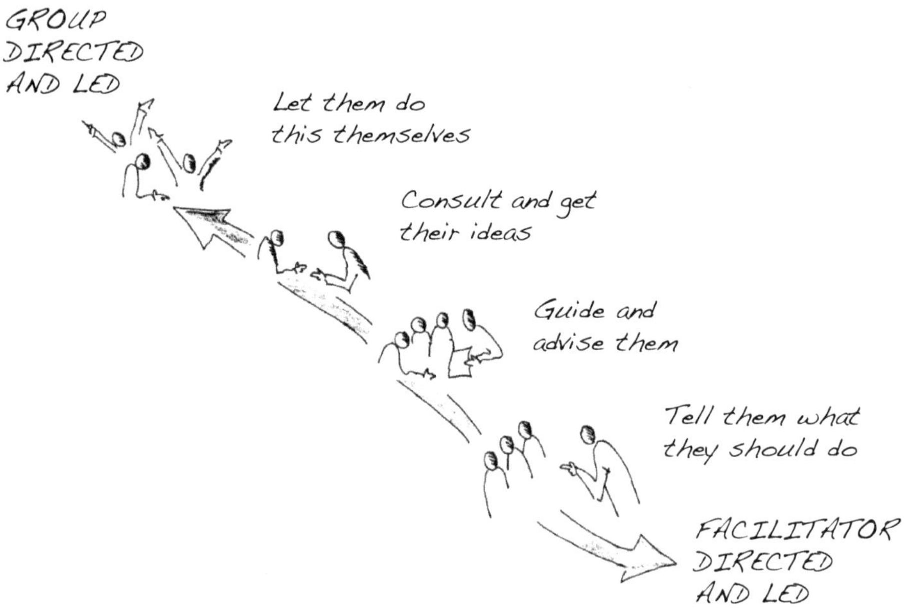

GROUP DIRECTED AND LED

Let them do this themselves

Consult and get their ideas

Guide and advise them

Tell them what they should do

FACILITATOR DIRECTED AND LED

This diagram above seeks to illustrate the levels of influence a facilitator has in working with a group. This is a sliding scale and the facilitator will adopt each of the stages on it at different times in the life of the group. However, the ideal is that over time, the facilitator's influence should move from being directive to supporting the group to do things for themselves. Similarly, the group over time should gain in confidence to make their own decisions and initiate new ideas and directions.

The basic level of influence is giving direction to what people do. This is appropriate in the early stages of a group coming together or at times when the group has lost a bit of direction or needs a bit of conflict resolution.

The next level is advice and guidance - this is less directive but the facilitator is still in control of the sort of advice and guidance that the group might need from him or her.

The next level is consultation, where the group can decide to accept or reject various options themselves.

The last level is when the group can decide for themselves and initiate new directions and ideas with very little outside help.

Edward de Bono's Six Thinking Hats
An aid to decision making and problem solving

The six thinking hat technique was developed by Edward de Bono and is a powerful tool that helps you look at important decisions from a number of different perspectives.

Hat thinking is a really good way of managing difficult discussions and decisions in a group. In some situations a few individuals dominate the discussion and when they express their feelings in a strong way it is sometimes difficult to see some of the facts and issues surrounding the discussion.

This method helps to structure the discussions according to a series of hats which represent key aspects that need to be covered in the discussion. The way it works is that the whole group think and discuss together according to the colour of the hat being suggested.

The White Hat

- The information seeking hat
- What are the facts?
- What information is available? What is relevant?
- When wearing the white hat we are neutral in our thinking

The Yellow Hat

- The sunshine hat
- It is positive and constructive
- It is about effectiveness and getting the job done
- What are the benefits, the advantages?

The Black Hat

- The caution hat
- In black hat the thinker points out errors or pit-falls
- What are the risks or dangers involved?
- Identifies difficulties and problems

The Red Hat

- What do you feel about the suggestion?
- What are your gut reactions?
- What intuitions do you have?
- Don't think too long or too hard

The Green Hat

- This is the creative mode of thinking
- Green represents growth and movement
- In green hat we look to new ideas and solutions
- Lateral thinking wears a green hat

The Blue Hat

- The control hat
- Used to help decide what other hats might be needed to help the decision making
- Allows the facilitator to reflect on how the group is working together
- Can be used to organise the next stage of discussion
- Acknowledges the group is stuck and might need a cup of tea or a beer!

For example, if the group was looking at a proposed idea they might want to use the white hat first to establish the facts, and then move on to the yellow and black hat which look at the advantages and disadvantages of the idea.

Once these have been discussed the facilitator could suggest looking at the red hat which allows everyone to express their feelings about the idea, before possibly looking at the green hat for alternative suggestions. If the group still cannot agree, the facilitator could use the blue hat to decide which of the hats the group needs to return to for further discussion.

Summary

Adair's three circles of leadership

John Adair's tool is a management tool but it is useful for a facilitator to bear in mind when working with a group on a particular task. A facilitator has to juggle three elements which are:

- Helping the group to make sure the task is achieved by giving them enough support when needed
- Managing the group energy and dynamics at the different stages of the Forming, Storming, Norming Performing cycle
- Managing individual needs and behaviours and ensuring full participation

The three circles in Adair's model overlap because:-

1. The task needs a team because one person alone cannot accomplish it.
2. If the team needs are not met the task will suffer and the individuals will not be satisfied.
3. If the individual needs are not met the team will suffer and performance of the task will be impaired.

Managing conflict

Conflict within a group can sabotage the process and severely limit a group's potential to achieve what it has set out to do. It is important for a facilitator to try to understand the cause of the behaviour as this is the first stage to addressing it. The iceberg illustration below suggests some causes of negative behaviour.

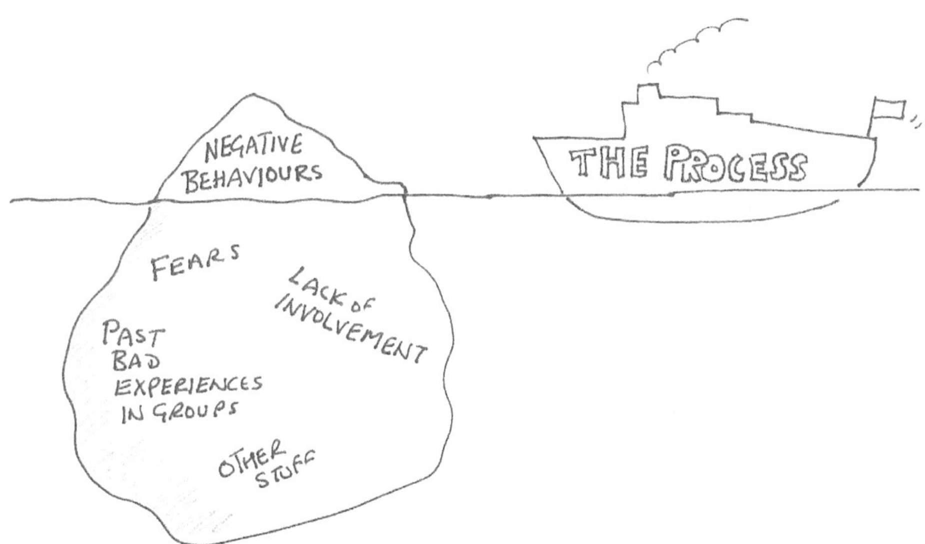

Stages of managing challenging behaviour

Difficult behaviour can be divided into two main categories, aggressive behaviour which can be disruptive and passive aggressive behaviour which is quiet or withdrawn.

These are suggested stages of managing challenging behaviour.

Stages of managing disruptive behaviour

Stage 1: Intentionally ignore

unhelpful/aggressive/distracting behaviour

Stage 2: Revisit ground rules

(e.g. mutual respect, no interrupting) Comments should be general referring to the group e.g. we need to listen to each other

Stage 3: Individual focus

e.g. "I can see you feel strongly about this - but we aren't able to address this here, we need to move on".

Stage 4: Private individual confrontation

"Your attitude is preventing the team from moving forward"

Stages of managing quiet and withdrawn behaviour

Stage 1

Initial attempt to draw individual out - open questions, eye contact, affirmation and encouragement

Stage 2

Discussion in pairs to get used to sound of own voice and opinions - affirm and encourage

Stage 3

Give them responsibility for a task to keep them engaged and cooperating with others

Stage 4

Ask them to feedback to the group on a particular task or issue if trust has been built and they are ready

Chairs

Purpose:

To show participants how to manage conflict by turning it into cooperation

Materials:

A chair for each participant or if it is a large group, limit the number of chairs to 20. Slips of paper with three instructions (see below)

Time: 30 minutes

Step-by-step guide:

1. Give a third of the participants instruction A, a third, instruction B and the final third instruction C. Tell them not to show their slip of paper to anyone. The three instructions are as follows:
   A Put all the chairs in a circle in the middle of the room
   B Put all the chairs by the door
   C Put all the chairs by the window
2. Tell everyone to start the exercise, following the instructions they have been given.

Comments:

This exercise has great scope for creative conflict resolution. Groups often burst into frantic action, using force and sometimes carrying chairs with others sitting on them. When some participants are trying to find a cooperative solution, others continue to defend their chairs.

After a while you may see participants try to come to a solution that keeps everyone happy, for example putting the chairs by the window, by the door and in a circle in the middle of the room consecutively.

Relevant questions for the analysis include:

1. What did you experience when playing this game?
2. Did you feel that the chair you were sitting on was yours to do with as you pleased?
3. How did you relate to people who wanted something else? Did you cooperate, persuade, argue, fight or give in?
4. Did you follow instructions? Did you see them as an instruction to be carried out whatever the cost and to the exclusion of others? Why?
5. In what ways are your feelings about instructions influenced by your cultural background? Has culture influenced the way you behaved in this situation?
6. How would you handle this exercise if you did it again?
7. Can you relate what happened here to real life situations?

DISC

In many cases, the cause of conflict can be attributed to a lack of understanding of another's point of view. The following model has four simple steps and begins by creating an understanding between the different parties before looking for solutions to resolve the conflict.

D

Describe the facts as each party in the conflict sees them

The facilitator should make sure that the facts are not distorted by too much emotion from either party.

I

What is the **impact** of that behaviour on each of the parties involved?

The facilitator should allow equal time for each party to describe how the conflict is affecting them. After both parties have spoken the facilitator should summarise what he or she has heard.

What possible **solutions** are there to solve this conflict?

The facilitator should help generate a range of solutions which are acceptable to all parties who then prioritise the best solutions.

What are the **consequences** of not reaching a solution to the problem?

If little progress is made while discussing possible solutions the facilitator should help both parties realise the consequences of not reaching a solution. This may include the effect on the wider community or relationships which are important for the future of any initiative or project. This should provide renewed energy for revisiting possible solutions.

Quotes on conflict resolution

"Every conflict we face in life is rich with positive and negative potential. It can be a source of inspiration, enlightenment, learning, transformation, and growth–or rage, fear, shame, entrapment, and resistance. The choice is not up to our opponents, but to us, and our willingness to face and work through them."
Kenneth Cloke and Joan Goldsmith

"If I were to summarise in one sentence the single most important principle I have learned in the field of interpersonal relations, it would be this: Seek first to understand, then to be understood. This principle is the key to effective interpersonal communication."
Stephen Covey

"Whenever you're in conflict with someone, there is one factor that can make the difference between damaging your relationship and deepening it. That factor is attitude."
William James

"Courage is what it takes to stand up and speak. Courage is also what it takes to sit down and listen."
Winston Churchill

Ten tips for creating a supportive environment

1. Create a sense of belonging in the group through energisers and fun exercises which bring the group together.
2. Use small groups to work on specific tasks or issues but make sure the group members are changed round regularly to avoid cliques or set patterns.
3. With shy members, encourage them to talk in pairs so they can feel more confident when talking in larger groups.
4. At regular intervals, as appropriate, check how the whole group is working and how it could be improved.
5. Check the pace and the energy of the group and if necessary, provide impromptu energisers.
6. Change the location to a different setting which could include the street, a café, a bus, garden, roof top.
7. Summarise where the group is so far and discuss with them the next steps.
8. Regularly invite the group to reflect on their learning and use creative methods to do this such as drama, posters and games.
9. Provide regular snacks and tasty food.
10. Encourage the group to affirm each other's contributions.

SECTION SEVEN

USE OF DRAMA AND ART IN FACILITATION

"If you want to be more creative stay in part a child, with the creativity and invention that characterises children before they are deformed by adult society."
Jean Piaget

Use of Drama

Many organisations use drama and role play as an essential element of their training programmes. The power of drama lies in recreating a relevant situation in a safe environment that people can watch, take part in, reflect on and discuss.

Drama sketches, monologues and mime can be used to highlight certain issues and problems which can then be discussed and acted upon.

Role play gives the opportunity for participants to enhance existing skills and develop new ones in a safe environment. This in turn will build confidence.

Drama or role play should be enjoyable, but at the same time, must be taken seriously to be effective. When this is the case, it can be the highlight of any training programme and a means through which much learning can take place.

"Theatre communicates with the whole person - not just with our thinking and reason. It appeals to our emotions, passions and prejudices."

"It is an entertaining way of sharing information. Both adults and children learn best when they are interested"

(From Footsteps issue no 58 "Theatre for Development" published by Tearfund)

"What I hear I forget, what I see I remember, what I do I understand"

Chinese proverb

Sketches

A sketch is a small scenario played out between 2 or more actors, the idea being to raise certain relevant issues in order to provoke discussion on those issues, with a view to learning how to manage them.

Tips for writing and performing sketches

1. Identify the issues that the sketch needs to bring out. What does the organisation need to address in the training?
2. Think of characters that could bring these issues out.
3. Think of a suitable scenario/setting.
4. It is helpful to write sketches in pairs, as two heads are better than one, and you have someone to exchange ideas with.
5. Try to include a humorous element. Humour is very powerful - sometimes built in around jargon, misunderstandings in procedures or because of the characteristics of the people in the sketch. Feel free to exaggerate the characters a little, although they should always be realistic.
6. One way of presenting certain issues is to make the sketch portray a negative situation involving those issues and asking the group to identify the problems and what could be done to address them.
7. After the sketch has been performed, ask your audience to discuss the issues they saw and how they would address them. Sometimes it is appropriate to draw up a list of principles, depending on what the subject matter is.
8. It is a good idea to present a sketch early in the proceedings as it can often drive the rest of the training. This also fits in with the adult learning cycle. Participants may well refer back to the sketch or the characters in it while taking part in activities later on in your training programme.

Monologues

A monologue is a stream of thought or reflections by one person. The idea is to present the characteristics of that person or the issues they are dealing with or both. Often these are easier than sketches to perform as there is no dependency on another person, and no need to remember cues. As long as you keep to the issues that need to be addressed you can vary the script.

Mime

A mime is a silent drama, often used to tell a story or to bring out certain principles. As there are no words, the body language and facial expressions can be exaggerated to make sure the audience knows what is going on.

Crossing the River

This is a mime (a silent drama) to help the community think about how to develop something for themselves and not be dependent on outside welfare support. Ask three participants to read through the activity and practise the mime. Then they can show it to the rest of the group and use the questions at the end for discussion.

Two lines fairly wide apart are drawn on the floor in chalk to represent the banks of the river. String can also be used if you do not want to draw on the floor. Pieces of paper are used to represent stepping stones and another large piece of paper is put in the middle of the river representing an island.

Two people come to the river and look for a place to cross. The current is very strong and they are both afraid to cross.

A third person comes along and sees their difficulty. He leads them up the river and shows them some stepping stones. He encourages them to use the stones but they are both afraid, so he agrees to carry one on his back.

By the time he gets to the middle of the river, the weight on his back seems very heavy, and he has become tired, so he puts the person down on the island.

The man goes back to get the other person on the bank who also wants to climb on his back. But the man refuses. Instead he takes her by the hand and encourages her to step on the stones herself.

Halfway across the river, she starts to manage alone. They both cross the river.

When they get to the other side, they are extremely pleased with themselves and they walk off together, completely forgetting the first man, alone on the island. He tries to get their attention, but they do not notice his frantic gestures for help.

Discussion questions

1. What did you see happening in the mime?
2. What different approaches were used to help the two people across?
3. Who could each person represent in real life?
4. What does each side of the river represent?
5. Why does this happen?
6. In what ways do community projects build a sense of dependence?
7. What must we do to ensure that those we work with develop a sense of independence?

Role Play

A role play is a simulation in which participants are required to act out the role of an individual in a situation or in circumstances that are relevant to the participants.

Role play is especially useful when you are training people in certain skills, particularly involving effective communication and inter-personal skills. Role play gives participants the opportunity to learn those skills in a completely safe environment.

Choosing a scenario

The choice is affected by three main factors:

- Credibility - must be familiar and recognised by the group
- Relevance - must portray the learning points required
- Level of complexity - must reflect the experience and understanding of the group

Checklist for conducting a role play

1. Explain the purpose of the session and the role play in particular. Outline the skills that should be practised.
2. Reassure participants - put them at their ease with the idea of role play.
3. Issue role play briefs or explain the scenario and then give sufficient time for preparation.
4. Select observers if appropriate.
5. Check everyone understands their role and be prepared to clarify and answer questions.
6. Start the role play and allow it to continue until a reasonable conclusion is reached, until the players dry up or no further progress is made or learning required.
7. Review the process. Allow players to speak first, then observers, then the trainer. Direct the discussion to cover the main learning points.
8. The trainer should close with a summary of what worked well, and what were the principal lessons and areas for all to concentrate on in the future.

Review and Feedback

Feedback should be:

- Balanced - it is important to recognise what worked well, as well as what didn't
- Specific - generalisations are not normally helpful. It should identify specific detail and the effect it caused
- Without judgment or speculation - stick to observable facts and their effects

Use of Film and TV Clips in Learning and Development

Film clips can be used in a similar way to sketches for either:

- Introducing a theme
- Demonstrating a relevant issue

Film clips have certain advantages over drama sketches.

- They are relatively easy to organise - no line learning or rehearsing required
- The clip is set in context - you don't have to imagine the setting
- Professional acting, directing and cinematography appeal to the whole person
- Participants may have already seen the film so can relate to it immediately
- You can put several film clips together in a sequence to enhance the effect

Tips when using film or tv clips

1. When introducing a film clip, make sure you describe its place within the context of the whole film and give the participants an idea of what they should be looking for.
2. Avoid technical difficulties by having the film set up before hand at exactly the right place, ready to play as soon as you've introduced it.
3. Check speakers and projector beforehand and make sure the sound quality is good.
4. Check the clip for language - make sure it is appropriate for your audience.
5. Be aware of any legal implications when using film clips. A licence may be required. In most cases, a film clip can be used with no licence, when it is being used for not for profit educational purposes.

The use of drawings and cartoons

There are many ways in which drawings and pictures can be used in facilitation. The three main ways are:

1. To communicate a message

Drawings say more than a thousand words, and many ideas and issues can be communicated through simple drawings or images. This is especially important to groups where literacy is very limited or where key messages need to be enhanced.

2. To provoke discussion

In this case, pictures are used to pose a problem or present an issue that a group can then analyse and discuss.

3. Therapeutic

Here, participants are encouraged to draw their experience or feelings about a particular situation or event. This has often been used with refugees or other people who have gone through a trauma or who have suffered a loss of some kind.

This section gives you some basic tips on how to draw simply but effectively.

Take a line for a walk

This is an important exercise as it helps to relax the wrist and allows you to draw lots of interesting shapes and patterns.

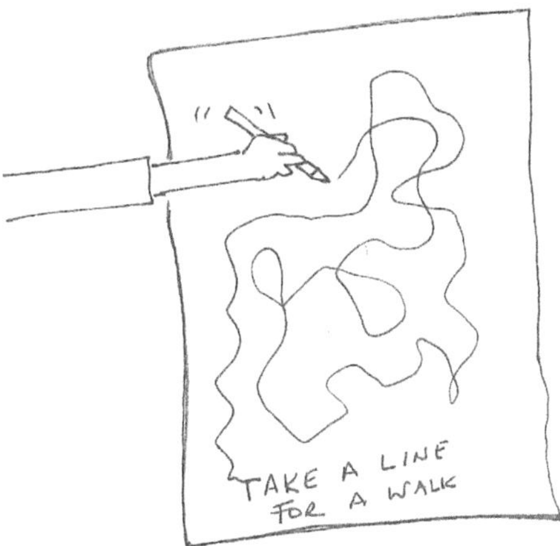

Now have a go at doing some doodles like the ones below.

The use of light to create shade

Shadows and shading help objects and people stand out more and also give a 3D effect which is sometimes useful.

1. Draw a circle and think of a light shining across it and consider where the shadow would fall.
2. The shadow would fall the opposite side from where the light is shining.

3. Experiment with different shapes. You will find the shadow helps to create a sense of depth.
4. Experiment by putting shadows at different angles and use different shapes.

Shadow people

Using this method it is now possible to create some simple figures using a combination of shapes and shadows. We call these shadow people, and these images are really useful for portraying difficult or sensitive subjects.

Drawing Faces

The advantage of drawing cartoon faces is that nothing has to be exactly right. However, it is sometimes useful to have a guide to build confidence. Below we have suggested some tips for drawing faces using grid lines which can be rubbed out once the face is drawn. Once you have practised this a few times you should be able to do it without the grid lines.

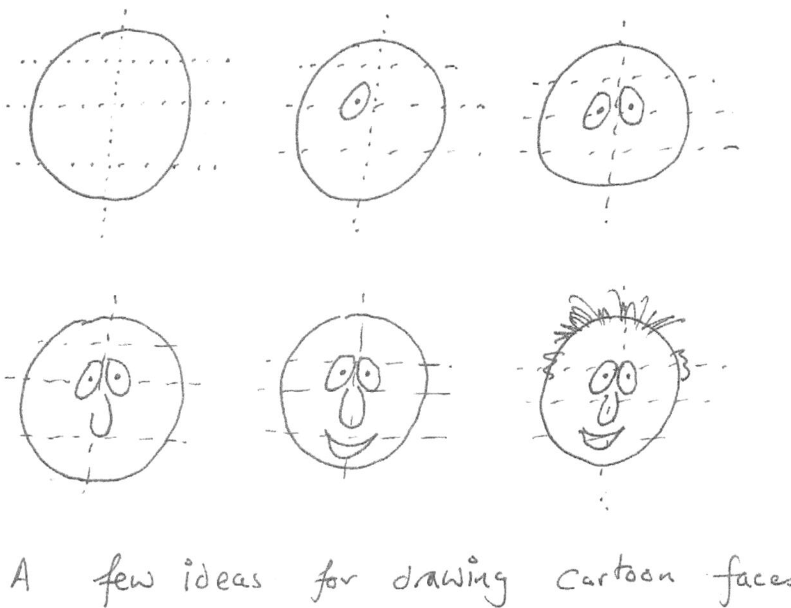

Try these:

How to make your flipcharts come alive

Flipcharts can look very dull so the following tips are designed to help you think about how you can liven them up using your new found drawing skills.

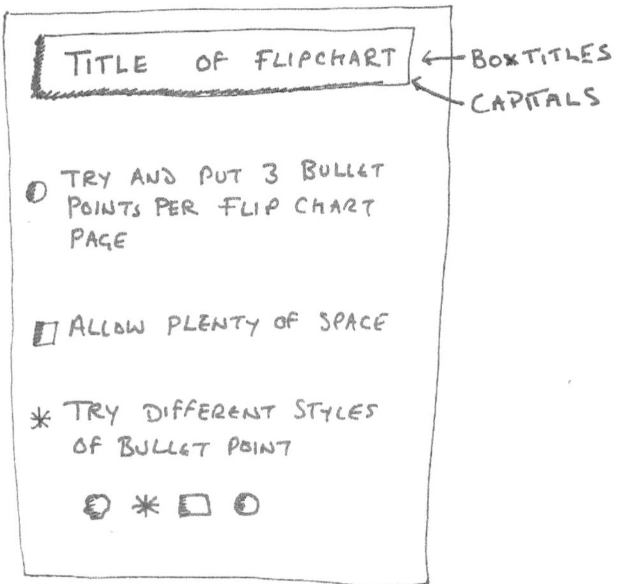

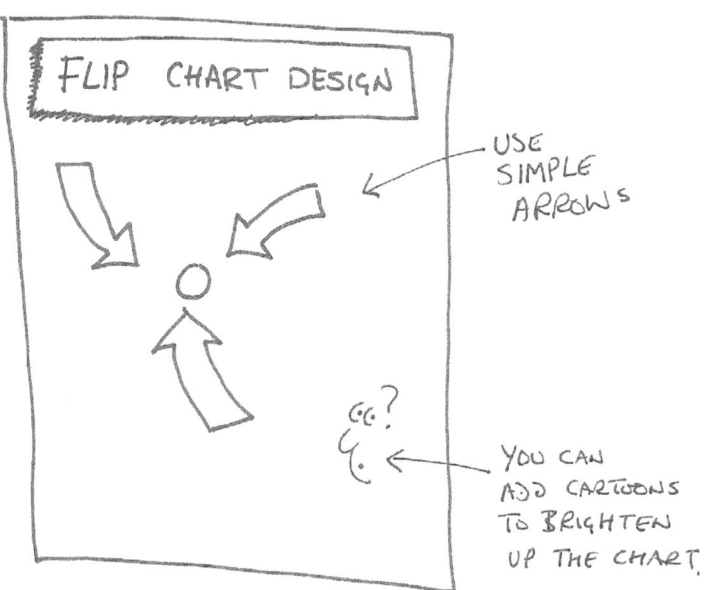

The advantage of using flipcharts is that you can explain a series of ideas one by one. Also, as you put them up, people can see the full picture and refer to the flipcharts during the session. Powerpoint does not allow for this. Once the slide has gone, it may be difficult for people to remember what they have seen.

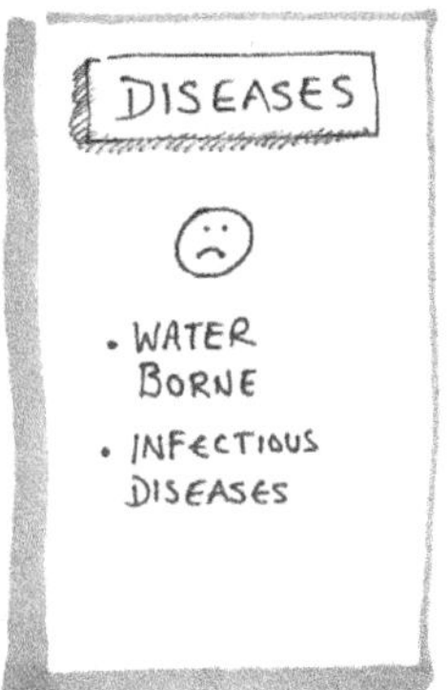

Being creative with rolls of paper

If you can get hold of large rolls of paper like lining paper or newsprint, you can make giant cartoon strips to explain a linear model or concept or even tell a story. As you roll out the paper, there is a sense of anticipation in the audience while the idea or story is being revealed.

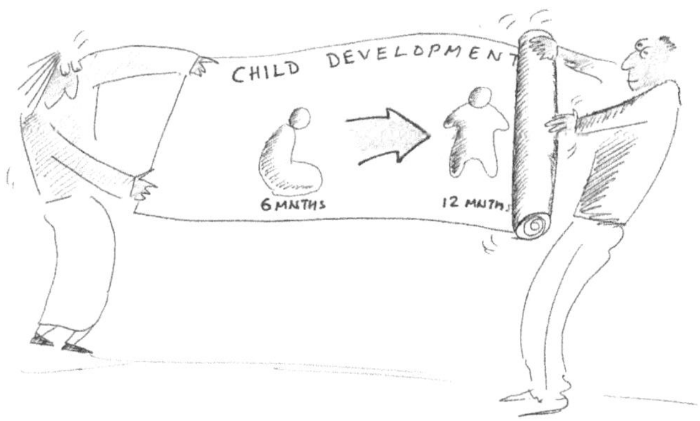

SECTION EIGHT

WORKING WITH YOUNG PEOPLE

Guiding principles for facilitators working with young people

1. **Be yourself**
   Try not to develop a rapport with young people by trying to be like them. They will accept you for who you are and not what you try to be.

2. **Work *with* young people - not *for* young people**
   (see ladder of participation on the next page) Young people are motivated to do things when they can decide for themselves. The role of the facilitator is to work with them in helping them discover their potential, and encouraging them to think through ways of realising it.
3. **Have fun!**
   Young people respond to humour and a sense of fun and will participate more if this is in plentiful supply.
4. **Go with the young people's energy**
   Young people get energised by things that are important to them and the role of the facilitator is to work with all the things that energise them in areas that are constructive and positive.
5. **Make listening a priority**
   Give young people your full attention when they are talking to you as this is a way of affirming and valuing them.

6. **React honestly to young people**
   Validate what young people say by reacting honestly to it. Agree or disagree and respect young people enough to explain why. Search for alternatives, if possible.

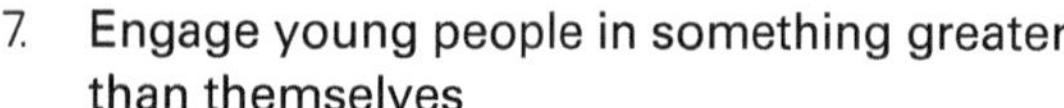

7. **Engage young people in something greater than themselves**
   Look for opportunities for them to do something challenging and ambitious that will make them feel they have achieved something beyond their perceived capability. This builds confidence and self esteem both as a group and as individuals.
8. **Use their creative energy**
   Young people are generally dynamic and creative and the facilitator should look for opportunities for them to express this in ways that are comfortable for them.

9. **Go for short term successes which they can feel proud of**
   To avoid feelings of failure and to give a sense of achievement, choose short term activities which will keep their interest and motivation.

The ladder of participation

Roger Hart UNICEF 1997

The ladder shows that the more you involve young people, the more ownership there is by them for what you are trying to do. The facilitator needs to be aware of what level he is engaging young people at and to think of ways of helping them take more responsibility.

Rung 8: Young people and adults share decision making

Rung 7: Young people lead and initiate action

Rung 6: Adult-initiated, shared decisions with young people

Rung 5: Young people are consulted and informed

Rung 4: Young people are assigned and informed

Rung 3: Young people are tokenised

Rung 2: Young people are decoration

Rung 1: Young people are manipulated

Degrees of participation

Rung of ladder	Description	Degree of participation
1	Manipulation	Adults use young people to support causes and pretend that the causes are inspired by young people.
2	Decoration	Young people are used to help a cause in a relatively indirect way, although adults do not pretend that the cause is inspired by young people.
3	Tokenism	Young people appear to be given a voice, but in fact have little or no choice about what they do or how they participate.
4	Assigned but informed	Young people are assigned a specific role and informed about how and why they are being involved.
5	Consulted and informed	Young people give advice on projects or programs designed and run by adults. The young people are informed about how their input will be used and the outcomes of the decisions made by adults.
6	Adult-initiated, shared decisions with young people	Projects or programs are initiated by adults but the decision-making is shared with the young people.
7	Young people initiated and directed	Young people initiate and direct a project or program.
8	Young people initiated, shared decisions with adults	Projects or programmes are initiated by young people and decision-making is shared between young people and adults. These projects empower young people while enabling them to learn from life experience and the expertise of adults.

Building a rapport

To effectively engage young people, allow time to build a rapport. This can take longer than you think but is ultimately worth it to gain their trust and interest.

- Consistency is important. Try to plan a regular time to meet which is no more than a week apart.
- Don't expect young people to come to you. Meet them at a place that is familiar to them.
- Let them lead the conversations and find out what things energise them. Take time to explore issues and dilemmas they have, even if they challenge your own values.
- Don't force your own value system on young people, but help them to work through their issues with open questions which help them to reflect on the consequences of their attitudes and actions.

"They simply need a reference point in the desert, the assurance of a friend for the future and ways to develop themselves without fear. Role models where love and care are seen and experienced as the norm."

Dave Wiles, Frontier Youth Trust, November 2009

PACE - (Play, Acceptance, Curiosity, Empathy)

This is a useful tip for thinking about the best way to relate to and work alongside young people and build relationships with them.

Play - young people like to be informal and enjoy joking around and respond well to an atmosphere that is relaxed and has a great sense of fun. Spontaneity and surprise will almost certainly go down well. Facilitators need to be ready to suggest activities that make people laugh and bring groups together.

Acceptance - young people need to know that they are accepted for who they are. This is important as it helps them feel significant and valued as human beings. This is a vital starting point for working with young people especially if they have had challenging and difficult childhood circumstances.

Curiosity - telling young people what they should and shouldn't do generally doesn't work as it sometimes reinforces their prejudice against authority. A far better option is to challenge their attitudes and behaviours through questions and being curious.

Empathy - facilitators need to be empathetic to young people's situations in order to help them feel that they have been listened to and understood. This builds their confidence and trust in sharing their experiences which, in turn, helps them to make sense of them.

SECTION NINE

ACTION LEARNING

Action learning

In an ideal situation, each facilitator would have somebody to support them. This is not always possible so action learning is a good alternative for creating support amongst peers.

Action learning is a powerful tool for helping individuals and groups solve complex and challenging problems. The process of action learning strengthens listening skills and the capacity to help people explore problems through the use of open questions. Being a member of a group can be a significant experience as trust between group members grows, and they are able to tackle significant issues together.

It is hoped that facilitators will use this action learning set method for supporting each other in addressing challenges they face as they work with different groups.

What is action learning?

Action learning is a structured method of enabling individuals to address complicated issues by meeting regularly and working together in small groups.

Key steps in action learning

- Each group member shares an issue or challenge they are facing.
- The other group members ask questions to help them reflect on their issue and explore ways of addressing the problem.
- The group helps each member to develop an action plan.
- At the next meeting everyone feeds back as to how they have got on and what they need further help on.

There are four main outcomes of the action learning set:

1. Each individual has successfully solved a challenge they came with.
2. Each individual has learned new insights from hearing the issues from other participants.
3. Each individual has improved in the way they listen to others, reflect on what they are saying and is better able to formulate the right questions to help someone.
4. As a group they have learned to trust each other and over time they are more effective in supporting and helping each other.

What are the core elements of action learning?

An action learning set involves 5 – 6 people meeting together on a regular basis. This can be every month or every six weeks, depending on the group needs and what they agree is appropriate. Young people such as teenagers, or vulnerable groups, may need to meet more frequently.

Each member of the action learning set identifies a challenge they are facing which they want to share with the group. The group then, through reflective questioning, helps the individual presenting the challenge to solve it for themselves.

Each member of the group takes it in turns to share their challenge by firstly, clarifying the challenge, secondly, exploring the challenge and some options to address it, and finally, developing some practical action which can be done before the group meets next time.

How does the group work?

The group is not to give advice or give the solution but to help each individual sharing their challenge to come up with their own solution.

An action learning set should have a facilitator who helps the group develop a structure of sharing, agreeing a code of conduct, and asking appropriate questions so the individuals can be helped to solve their own problems.

Key steps of action learning

1. Identify a challenge or problem you would like the group to help you with.
2. Share it with the group so they can ask questions to help you explore and understand the problem.
3. The group helps you gain a new insight and plan of action to address part or all of the problem.
4. Test out the plan of action and see if it makes any difference.
5. Review what happened. Draw lessons from the experience and continue to apply them to your work.

Structuring an action learning set

This diagram is a rough guide to show how long each person should have to explore their issue(s). In general most groups give each member 45 – 60 minutes air time.

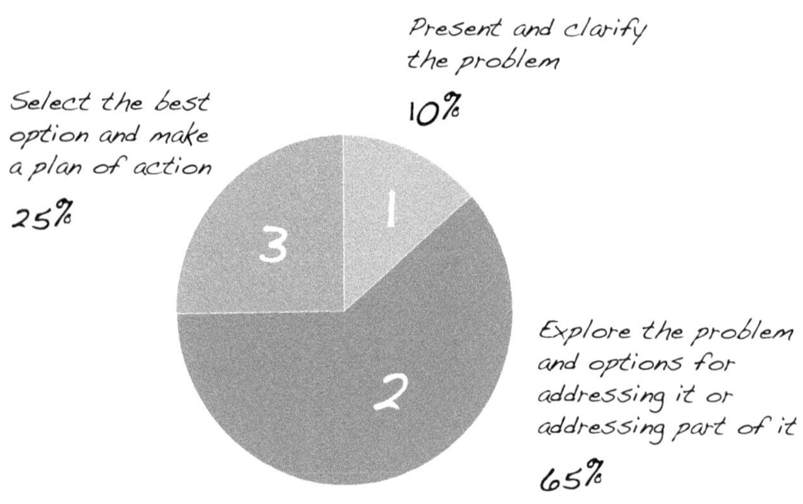

How do we structure the action learning sharing?

This table is just a guide to help you think about how you might structure this group session. As a suggestion, groups could meet for half a day which allows 30 minutes per session and also breaks and time at the end to review all the actions everyone is going to take.

If group members have more time, it may be appropriate to lengthen the time of each session and spend a whole day together.

Timing	Sessions	Tips for the facilitators
	Welcome and introduction	Make this warm and friendly
15 - 20 minutes	Review the purpose of the group Review the ground rules	
	Start the action learning. Clarify that each person will have half an hour and there will be a break between each person sharing	
5 - 10 minutes	Sharing of the challenge	Ensure the group uses clarifying type questions
10 - 20 minutes	Exploring options and deepening understanding	Ensure use of exploring questions
5 - 10 minutes	Action planning	Ensure action orientated questions
	Reflect on how the group worked. Is there any room for improvement?	Facilitator to make a note of the feedback and to ensure improvements are made
Repeat the above cycle for the next 4 people, taking breaks when the group needs them.		

Action learning set review form

This review form is to be used by all the participants in the set to review both their individual and the group's progress over their time together.

Key areas for assessing progress	After first meeting	After several meetings (what changes have you noticed since the meetings started)	Review after many meetings (What has been achieved as a result of these meetings? What practical things have you done? What new insights have you gained?)
How has the group encouraged you and helped you?			
Which areas are you improving in? • Listening skills • Asking questions • Preparing for the meeting • Presenting a challenge or problem			
How is the group working to support each other?			
What is the group learning together about action learning sets?			

Things that need to be decided in meeting as an action learning set

- How often shall we meet?
- Where shall we meet? and for how long?
- How shall I go about identifying a challenge and preparing to share it in the group next time?
- Are there any remaining fears or concerns we need to address?

APPENDICES

Appendix 1: Checklist for assessing and developing facilitation skills

This is a useful checklist to help you review your facilitation skills. You could go through these questions on your own or with a group of facilitators.

- How did I make people feel relaxed and welcome?
- How relevant was the information I shared to the group using it? How did I adapt the information so that it was relevant to the group?
- How did I encourage quiet members of the group to participate?
- How did I deal with differences of opinion?
- How did I deal with people who dominated the group discussion?
- How did I respond to questions from members of the group? Was I able to answer them? If not, how could I find out more information that would help me deal with future questions?
- How did I introduce the discussion? How could I have done this better?
- How did I encourage further discussion?
- How did I deal with sensitive issues?
- Did I bring the discussion to a satisfactory conclusion?
- How could I have done this better?
- How did I ensure the group's ideas were recorded for use in future discussion, group planning or for sharing with others?
- Did group members make any decisions about how to put learning into practice? If not, how could I encourage this?
- What additional information or follow-up discussion is needed in order to address underlying views and attitudes to the topics discussed?

Appendix 2: Resources

If I keep an open mind, will my brain fall out?
Anon

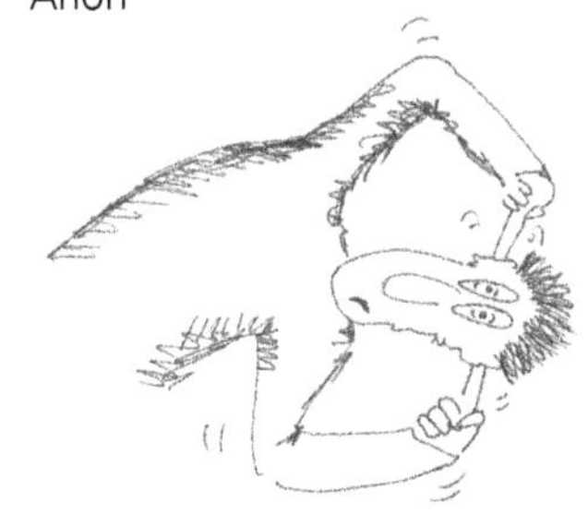

Getting things done when you are not in charge
Geoffrey M Bellman
Berrett-Koehler Publishers, Inc

Participatory Learning and Action - A Trainer's Guide
Jules N Pretty, Irene Guijt, John Thompson, Ian Scoones
IIED

Action Learning - A Practical Guide
Krystyna Weinstein
Gower Publishing Ltd

Facilitator's Guide to Participatory Decision-Making
Sam Kaner
New Society Publishers

People and Change - Exploring Capacity-Building in NGOs
Rick James
INTRAC

A Rough Guide to Change
Jenny Hyatt
Charities Evaluation Services

Facilitating Learning - A sourcebook of activities
Tony Spinks Phil Clements
Viva Books Private Ltd

The World Café: Shaping our Futures Through Conversations that Matter
Juanita Brown with David Isaacs and the World Café Community
(Berrett-Koehler, 2005)

Institute for Outdoor Learning
www.outdoor-learning.org

About Mosaic Creative

We are a small training consultancy, working mainly in the field of community development, both in the UK and internationally, specialising in the use of drama, cartoons and illustrations to enhance learning and development.

Our approach is about provoking a reaction, communicating ideas, exploring meaning and unlocking the creative potential in others. Mosaic Creative has an in house capacity to design and produce its own publications as well as tailor-made resources for clients.

Bill Crooks

Bill has worked with the not for profit sector for over 25 years, both in the UK and internationally, running courses on a wide range of community development issues. He is an accomplished cartoonist and illustrator and uses these skills to powerful effect in his training courses and workshops. This includes the use of graphic facilitation for capturing learning from conferences and strategic events. He has written and illustrated many community development resources, currently being used in the UK and internationally.

Jackie Mouradian

Jackie is a professional actor, script writer and facilitator, working with both the corporate and charity sectors, especially in the context of organisational change and development. She writes and performs in sketches relevant to the needs of the company or organisation and provides meaningful and realistic environments within which effective learning can take place. She also co-writes community development resources for use in the UK and internationally.

Lindsay Noble

Lindsay's graphic design work at Mosaic Creative focuses on developing accessible, user-friendly and exciting designs for resource materials used in a variety of cross cultural settings.

For further details, please contact:

info@mosaiccreative.co.uk
www.mosaiccreative.co.uk

www.ingramcontent.com/pod-product-compliance
Ingram Content Group UK Ltd.
Pitfield, Milton Keynes, MK11 3LW, UK
UKHW051128260726
13967UKWH00010B/2926